ANIMALS THAT TRAVEL

THINGS ANIMALS DO

Kyle Carter

The Rourke Book Co., Inc.
Vero Beach, Florida 32964

Edited by Sandra A. Robinson and Pamela J.P. Schroeder

PHOTO CREDITS
All photos © Kyle Carter

Library of Congress Cataloging-in-Publication Data

Carter, Kyle, 1949-
    Animals that travel / by Kyle Carter.
    p. cm. — (Things animals do)
    Includes index.
    ISBN 1-55916-110-8
    1. Animal migration—Juvenile literature. [1. Animals—Migration.] I. Title. II. Series: Carter, Kyle, 1949-   Things animals do.
QL754.C335 1995
591.52'5—dc20   94-47360
                                                 CIP
                                                 AC

Printed in the USA

TABLE OF CONTENTS

ANIMALS THAT TRAVEL

Certain animals regularly make long journeys each year, usually in the spring and fall.

These journeys are among nature's greatest events. Thousands of animals become restless with the change of seasons and begin to move. Great clouds of birds take flight, and herds of grazing animals travel from one season's homeland to another.

True travelers—scientists call them **migrants**—make their journeys at about the same time each year. They travel to and from the same places each year.

The golden plover nests on the Arctic tundra, then flies 8,000 miles to its winter home in Argentina

FALL TRAVEL

Each fall the green plants that many animals eat quit growing. The crowd of insects that are tasty food for larger animals dies, hides away or flies south. Most leaves, berries and seeds disappear under a blanket of snow. Ice locks up ponds and lakes. Food becomes scarce.

Few animals live well during the winter. Many animals avoid the hardships of winter by traveling to a place where winter weather is milder. There the animals can find plenty of food.

Tundra swans leave the Far North in September and fly to winter homes in mild California, Virginia and North Carolina

SPRING TRAVEL

In early spring, the migrant animals begin to travel again. In North America, most of them journey from the south to the north. They return to summer homes to raise families.

Spring travel can be difficult to understand. Why should snow geese, for example, leave a winter home where food is plentiful? These birds have to fly hundreds of miles north to reach nesting grounds on the grassy **tundra** of Canada.

Snow geese begin their journey north to the Arctic tundra in early spring

THE TRAVEL HABIT

Part of the reason that birds like snow geese fly north is **tradition,** or habit. Traditions are activities that are repeated year after year. People have traditions, such as decorating Christmas trees. Animals have traditions, too. Snow geese are doing what they have done for thousands of years—traveling with the seasons.

Long ago the Earth's climate was different. Perhaps then the snow geese *had* to journey great distances, and their tradition of travel began.

Traveling caribou follow the same routes their parents and grandparents did

Traveling sockeye salmon return to the streams where they were born, to lay eggs and die (see title page photo)

Animal travel is full of risks, like the fast-moving current
these wildebeests are battling

WHY ANIMALS TRAVEL

Tradition is a strong force. Tradition, though, is not the only reason that geese and other animals travel long distances each fall.

The kinds of food an animal eats at its summer home are different than its winter foods. Some animals may need to change the kinds of food they eat to stay healthy.

The summer home may offer safer, better places to raise young and relief from the heat, too.

The Canadian tundra is an ideal nesting place for snow geese

WHO TRAVELS …

Birds are the best-known travelers, although not all **species,** or kinds, of birds travel with the seasons.

Millions of birds—about 400 species—travel each year through North America alone. They fly up and down the continent along invisible paths in the sky called flyways. Birds on **seasonal** flights remind people that the seasons are changing.

Sea turtles, seals, penguins and fish travel long distances through the oceans. Birds and monarch butterflies travel far through the air. Herds of wildebeests in Africa and caribou in North America travel across wide plains.

Wildebeests, following the rains and good grass, travel across the plains of East Africa

… AND WHO DOESN'T?

Seasonal travel isn't for every animal. Some animals escape winter through a deep sleep called **hibernation.** Four-legged **predators** such as wolves may have to travel to find food, but they do not make regular seasonal journeys.

Birds that are not strong fliers, such as wild turkeys and pheasants, *can't* travel long distances. Some birds—and mammals, too—survive winter by searching for acorns and other plant leftovers.

In certain groups of animals, some travel and others don't. Traveling killer whales pass through seas in British Columbia where other killer whales live year-round.

A pod of killer whales cruises through Johnston Strait, British Columbia, in search of salmon

HOW ANIMALS TRAVEL

Long-distance animal travel is full of mystery. Scientists are just beginning to unlock its secrets.

Birds probably use the stars and landmarks on the ground, such as rivers, to help guide their flights. That helps explain how an Arctic tern can make a 25,000-mile round-trip from the Arctic to the Antarctic.

Adult salmon return to the streams where they were born. They must be able to sense the special smell of their home stream.

Perched on a rock in the Arctic, this tern will travel 12,500 miles in autumn to the Antarctic, where it will be spring

TRAVEL MYSTERIES

Animals have many senses and abilities for travel that humans don't have. It is still a mystery how many of these animal abilities work.

For example, monarchs travel each fall from the United States and southern Canada south into the mountains of central Mexico. These monarchs were born in late summer. Not one has ever been to Mexico before! How do they find their winter homes?

Sea turtle travel is another mystery. Somehow they find their way across thousands of miles of open sea to their home beaches.

Glossary

hibernation (hi ber NAY shun) — the deep, sleeplike state in which certain animals survive the winter

migrant (MY grihnt) — an animal that makes a long journey at about the same time and to the same place each year

predator (PRED uh tor) — an animal that hunts another animal for food

seasonal (SEEZ un ul) — referring to something that is done regularly during the same season each year

species (SPEE sheez) — within a group of closely-related animals, one certain kind, such as a *snow* goose

tradition (truh DISH un) — an activity that is repeated year after year at the same time and place

tundra (TUN druh) — the treeless carpet of low-lying plants in the Far North and on mountains above the tree line

INDEX